D0633073

Owlkids Books acknowledges the financial support of the Canada Council for the Arts, the Ontario Arts Council, the Government of Canada through the Canada Book Fund (CBF) and the Government of Ontario through the Ontario Media Development Corporation's Book Initiative for our publishing activities.

Published in Canada by
Owlkids Books Inc.
10 Lower Spadina Avenue
Toronto, ON M5V 2Z2

Published in the United States by
Owlkids Books Inc.
1700 Fourth Street
Berkeley, CA 94710

Cataloguing data available from Library and Archives Canada.

ISBN 978-1-77147-105-3 (bound)

Library of Congress Control Number: 2015948454

Edited by: Karen Li
Designed by: Diane Robertson

Canada

ONTARIO ARTS COUNCIL
CONSEIL DES ARTS DE L'ONTARIO
an Ontario government agency
un organisme du gouvernement de l'Ontario

Canada Council
for the Arts
Conseil des Arts
du Canada

Manufactured in Dongguan, China, in November 2015, by Toppan Leefung Packaging & Printing (Dongguan) Co., Ltd.

Job #BAYDC19

A   B   C   D   E   F

Publisher of Chirp, chickaDEE and OWL
www.owlkidsbooks.com

Owlkids Books is a division of  Bayard
C A N A D A

SOURCES AND ACKNOWLEDGMENTS

The author consulted the websites of the following organizations while researching this book: Adelaide Zoo (Australia), Auckland Zoo (New Zealand), Bat World Sanctuary (Texas), Berlin Zoo (Germany), Brandywine Zoo (Delaware), Bristol Zoo (England), The Elephant Sanctuary (Tennessee), Fort Worth Zoo (Texas), Fresno Chaffee Zoo (California), Honolulu Zoo (Hawaii), Lincoln Park Zoo (Illinois), Lucknow Zoo (India), Monterey Bay Aquarium (California), Nashville Zoo (Tennessee), National Aviary (Washington, D.C.), Performing Animal Welfare Society (PAWS) (California), Phoenix Zoo (Arizona), Pittsburgh Zoo & PPG Aquarium (Pennsylvania), San Diego Zoo (California), Seafood Watch, Seneca Park Zoo (New York), Tampa's Lowry Park Zoo (Florida), Taronga Zoo (Australia), Tiergarten Schönbrunn (Austria), Woodlawn Park Zoo (Washington), World Wildlife Fund, and Zoo Atlanta (Georgia).

With special thanks to the following zoos for providing additional information and interviews: Arizona-Sonora Desert Museum (Arizona), Birch Aquarium (California), Chester Zoo (England), Lone Pine Koala Sanctuary (Australia), Saint Louis Zoo (Missouri), Toronto Zoo (Ontario).

WORMS for BREAKFAST

HOW TO FEED A ZOO

Written by Helaine Becker

Illustrated by Kathy Boake

Owlkids Books

It's feeding time at the zoo—and *you're* in charge. What should you put on your menagerie's menu? If only you had a recipe book, one that could show you how to feed all your animal friends…

But wait! You do!

With this book in hand, you can satisfy the hungriest of hippos and the greediest of gorillas. You'll be able to whip up a feast for bats and wombats alike. You'll also find out about some of the challenges zookeepers face in taking care of so many different animals.

So let's get cooking!

PLATYPUS PARTY MIX

Platypuses store extra food in cheek pouches while under water. Once they surface, it's snack time!

YOU WILL NEED
10–15 live crayfish
1 oz. (30 g) live earthworms
⅓ oz. (10 g) live mealworms
1 tsp. (5 mL) live fly pupae

1. Mix all ingredients in a large bowl and serve immediately. If platypuses are still hungry, give them another wriggly helping of earthworms and mealworms before bed.

Menu

Hungry, Hungry Hippos...and More!

Some animals, like lions, only eat meat. These animals are called carnivores. Others only eat plants. These are called herbivores. Insectivores only eat insects. Frugivores only eat fruit. What about humans? We are omnivores. That means we eat, well, anything and everything! Bears, skunks, and raccoons are also omnivores.

How do zookeepers keep up with all these different diets? To begin, they focus less on the types of food each animal eats in the wild and more on the nutrients it needs. For example, all animals need calcium to build healthy bones. So zoo nutritionists make sure every animal gets the right amount of calcium in its diet, as well as other vitamins and minerals.

Of course, it doesn't matter how healthy the food is if animals won't eat it. Giraffes, for example, need to eat a high-fiber diet. That means hay, hay, and more hay. But once in a while, a sprig of willow or poplar makes mealtime more fun. The chewy twigs are also good for giraffes' teeth—like an all-natural toothbrush.

MENU MANIA

Different animals eat different kinds of foods. These lunches got all mixed up. Match each delish dish below with the animal that would want to dig in! Answers are on page 32.

GORILLA GOBBLE-'EM-UPS

Guess who goes gaga for these crunchy, carroty cookies?

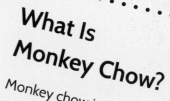

YOU WILL NEED

1 cup (250 mL) boiled carrots

½ cup (125 mL) oatmeal

1 cup (250 mL) monkey chow

1 egg, beaten

1 tbsp. (15 mL) wheat germ

dried ants to taste

1. Preheat oven to 350°F (180°C).

2. Puree carrots.

3. Use a food processor to finely grind oatmeal with monkey chow.

4. Stir carrots into oat mixture until smooth.

5. Add egg and mix well.

6. Add wheat germ and mix well.

7. Roll dough into balls, flatten, and sprinkle each cookie with ants. Bake in the oven for approximately 12 to 15 minutes, until golden brown.

What Is Monkey Chow?

Monkey chow is a dry, commercially prepared animal food. It's a lot like dog biscuits or kitty kibble, but it's made for primates. Like many animals at the zoo, primates have a less varied diet than they would in the wild. Monkey chow contains grains, fats, proteins, and other nutrients to round out their zoo menu.

5

Kitchen Capers

Zoo animals eat A LOT! At the Brandywine Zoo in Wilmington, Delaware, the weekly grocery list for proteins alone can include 280 lb. (125 kg) of meat, 4 lb. (1.8 kg) of fish, 60 eggs, 500 crickets, 1,000 mealworms, 35 rats, and 50 mice! Join some chefs in a typical zoo kitchen to see what ingredients are used and how they're prepared.

Binders of recipes help chefs prepare the food properly.

Meet a Zoo Nutritionist

Who: Jap Wensvoort, Lead Nutritionist

Where: Toronto Zoo, Toronto, Ontario

Favorite part of the job: I love the diversity and challenge. At the Toronto Zoo, my team prepares 500 different animal diets daily! I love working with all these different animal species and all the different people who work here, too. In 2014, the Toronto Zoo celebrated 40 years of saving and protecting animals and their habitats at home and abroad. I am proud to be a part of that.

Favorite human foods: Seafood, curries, meat and potatoes, and chocolate.

Keeping the kitchen clean is a top priority. Chefs must dunk their shoes in a basin of disinfectant when they enter.

Even animals have to take their vitamins!

Because different foods keep best at different temperatures, the kitchen has multiple freezers and refrigerators. Each may be set at a temperature ranging from 41°F (5°C) to –22°F (–30°C).

Food is carefully weighed on scales. Each animal receives 2–4% of its body weight in food a day.

Each animal gets a takeout bin or tray labeled with its name.

Nutritional biscuits are stored nearby in bins. These can be added as needed to each animal's meal.

Separate work areas are used to prepare food for different types of animals.

Babying the Kids

Cuter-than-cute animals are being born all the time in zoos. The best way to feed animal babies is the natural way. For mammals, that means letting Mama do it! Most of the mammal babies born in zoos are nursed by their mothers. That way, they get the perfect food, in the right quantities, at the right time.

Nursing mothers need extra care themselves if their babies are to grow big and strong. Zookeepers look after new moms by feeding them calorie-rich treats. This gives them the energy they'll need to make milk for their babies.

LENDING A HELPING HAND

Sometimes zoo moms and dads aren't able to care for their babies. They might not know how, or they might not be healthy enough to do it on their own. That's when zoo staff step in. For example, when a swamp wallaby was rejected by her mother at Australia's Taronga Zoo, keepers took over. They fed the joey, named Mirrawa, a special formula created just for wallabies. As she grew, she was hand-fed soft new leaves of local plants like bottlebrush. To help her feel at home, a zookeeper kept Mirrawa inside a cuddly pouch, worn on the front of the keeper's body day and night.

FLAMINGO CHICK FORMULA

Flamingos use their curved beaks like a sieve to filter bits of food out of the water. But baby flamingos are born with straight beaks! In the wild, parents feed chicks until their beaks change shape. At the zoo, keepers do the feeding with this protein-rich slush.

YOU WILL NEED

¾ lb. (340 g) small oily fish (such as smelt or capelin), beheaded, finned, and diced

4 cups (1000 mL) water

¾ lb. (340 g) shrimp, peeled and diced

17 yolks from hardboiled eggs

¾ lb. (340 g) cooked rice cereal

½ cup (125 mL) vitamin powder

1. In a blender, puree diced fish with 1 cup (250 mL) water. Over a large bowl, pour fish puree into a strainer and push through with a spatula to remove any lumps.

2. Puree shrimp with 1 cup (250 mL) water. Pour shrimp puree into a strainer over the same bowl and push through with a spatula to remove lumps.

3. Puree egg yolks, rice cereal, and vitamin power with 2 cups (500 mL) water. Pour egg puree into a strainer over the same bowl and push through with a spatula to remove lumps.

4. Stir all three purees together, and then return the mixture to the blender for a final puree.

5. For younger chicks, heat the formula in a microwave to flamingo body temperature before serving it to them from a syringe. Extra Flamingo Chick Formula can be refrigerated or frozen for later use.

A Recipe for Conservation

Some zoo animals are endangered or very rare. Zookeepers offer the babies of endangered animals extra care to give the species the best chance of survival. At the Adelaide Zoo in Australia, a rare palm cockatoo egg was removed from its parents' nest. The two birds had never been able to successfully raise hatchlings before. So zookeepers placed the egg in an incubator (a machine that keeps eggs warm) until it hatched.

For the first few weeks of its life, the hatchling needed feeding every hour and a half. Keepers took turns taking it home overnight! At two months, the chick needed to be fed only twice a day. It could then stay at the zoo full time.

THE MYSTERY OF THE CLOUDED LEOPARD

Even with extra care, not all endangered zoo animals survive. For example, less than half the clouded leopard cubs born in zoos grow up to be adults. The mothers often ignore or injure their cubs, but no one really knows why. Clouded leopards are vulnerable–and extremely secretive–creatures, so there is little information about how they behave in the wild.

To keep newborn cloud leopard cubs safe, keepers usually "pull" them (separate them from their mothers) at birth. When they do this, the number of cubs that survive more than doubles. The caregivers first feed cubs a milk-based

formula made specially for zoo cats. When the cubs are about a month old, pureed turkey is added to their formula. This makes the meal more nutritious and gives the cubs a taste for meat. Gradually the keepers add more and more meat until the bottles contain a "meat milkshake"!

Zookeepers feed and burp the cubs, but otherwise handle them as little as they can. This keeps the cubs as wild as possible so that they may one day be reintroduced to their natural habitats.

HELLO, SLOW FOOD!

The Partula snail is extinct in the wild. Only a handful survive in zoos around the world. Some of these zoos—such as the Bristol Zoo in England and the Woodlawn Park Zoo in Seattle, Washington—take special care to raise Partula snail babies. They hope to increase the number of these snails and one day restore them to their natural habitats.

SNAIL TRAIL MIX

Partula snails have tiny mouths, so their food needs to be even tinier. This recipe yields a finely ground slurry, so supper is slurp-ready.

YOU WILL NEED

1 tsp. (5 mL) oats
1 tsp. (5 mL) dried grass
1 tsp. (5 mL) fish pellets
1 tsp. (5 mL) ground cuttlefish bone

1. In a small food processor or blender, mix all ingredients together.

2. Add a few drops of water, as needed, so the mixture forms a paste.

3. Serve by smearing the paste onto the inside of the snails' tank.

11

Midnight Snacks

In the wild, nocturnal animals wake up at sunset—with growling tummies! How do keepers feed animals that sleep all day? At the Berlin Zoo in Germany, they beat the clock with a "trick of the light." In the morning, they dim lights in nocturnal animal exhibits to simulate moonlight. This makes nocturnal animals think it's nighttime. At night, when the rest of the zoo grows dark, these cages light up, letting both keepers and nocturnal animals rest easy. The animals wake up at "sunset," ready to have their breakfast at the same time as the zoo's early risers.

See what a "midnight" raid on the fridge might yield for night owls—and other animals that are active after dark.

❶ **OWL BOWL-O'-FUN**: At the Lincoln Park Zoo in Chicago, Illinois, eastern screech owls are fed one live mouse a day.

❷ **STINKY'S STEW**: Skunks are omnivores, so they enjoy a mixture of meat and veg, including cooked ground chicken, brown rice, barley, and rolled oats.

❸ **PANGOLIN POTAGE**: Wild pangolins use their extra-long, extra-sticky tongue to snag ants and termites. At California's San Diego Zoo, these scaly creatures lap up a soup made of blended meat, protein mix, and food pellets for insectivores.

❹ **SUGAR GLIDER FRUITY SALAD SURPRISE**: Sugar glider possums love fruit, fruit, and more fruit. This sweet treat layers a mixture of fruit with rice cereal. It's sprinkled with dog kibble and fly pupae for extra protein.

❺ **CECAL PELLETS**: Rabbits eat their own poop! Really! It's an important part of their diet. Overnight or in the early morning, rabbits poop special "night feces." Eating them gives the bunnies—which are herbivores—extra nutrients.

❻ **JUNGLE SMOOTHIE**: Sometimes fruit bats simply squash up their favorite fruits and slurp up the sweet juice. It's an all-natural jungle smoothie!

❼ **FOX CANDY**: Bat-eared foxes get a mixed diet of dog food, mice, crickets, and mealworms. They love mealworms so much that keepers at the San Diego Zoo call them fox candy!

Did You Know?

Mealworms aren't worms at all. They are the larvae of the darkling beetle. Zoos buy them packed in boxes of grain. Inside the boxes, some of the larvae will have started to change into pupae (the next stage of the insect's life, before it becomes a beetle). Bats don't like pupae, so keepers separate them out. The best method? Letting the mealworms do it themselves! At Bat World Sanctuary in Weatherford, Texas, the keepers shine a light over one end of their kitchen storage bin. Larvae hate light, so they crawl to the shady side. *Voilà*! Self-sorted snacks!

The Thrill of the Hunt

In the wild, animals don't find bowls of breakfast ready and waiting each morning. Predators like lions and tigers must chase and capture their food before chowing down. Without the thrill of the hunt, zoo animals might get bored or lazy. They might overeat, or lose their appetites entirely.

Zookeepers work hard to keep this from happening. They change predators' feeding routines often so the animals never know what to expect. And they make meals that require some effort–animals must find the food or wrestle it from hard-to-open containers. This keeps peckish predators healthy and happy.

An unusual smell can be enough to give predators a thrill. At the Pittsburgh Zoo in Pennsylvania, the big cat enclosure is sometimes scented with allspice or elephant manure. The unfamiliar smell keeps the cats alert and curious for hours!

Meet a Zoo Nutritionist

Who: Dr. Deb Schmidt, Nutritionist

Where: St. Louis Zoo, St. Louis, Missouri

Favorite part of the job: The fun part of being an animal nutritionist is helping to solve problems. I like to figure out what nutrients animals need and at what levels. Sometimes domestic animals (like cows, horses, chickens, dogs, or cats) give us clues about what wild animals similar to them may need. But the diets of other animals (such as apes and reptiles) can be harder to figure out.

Special skills needed: To be a zoo nutritionist, you should be good in math and have a strong background in sciences like biology and biochemistry. Then you typically need a university degree in animal or human nutrition.

PREDATOR POPSICLE

Serve this frosty favorite to felines on hot days for buckets of fun.

YOU WILL NEED
1 large animal bone (deer or cow)
5 gal. (20 L) bucket of water

1. Place bone in water and store in freezer until water is frozen solid.

2. Remove ice (with bone) from bucket. It is now a predator popsicle!

3. Float popsicle in the tiger enclosure's pond, like an iceberg. Watch tigers study, fetch, lick, gnaw, and play with their frosty treat all day long.

Did You Know?

In the wild, predators don't eat every day. That's why Thursdays at the Fort Worth Zoo in Texas are fasting days for jaguars. They receive only bones.

Brain Food

Foraging animals like chimpanzees and elephants also need to search for their supper in the wild. The search exercises their bodies—and their minds. Foragers might have to figure out how to reach an underground nest or crack a hard-to-open shell. Remembering where to find fave foods also delivers a big brain workout.

To challenge foragers to use their brains, zookeepers sometimes hide food in creative ways. At the Auckland Zoo in New Zealand, hollow balls filled with diced fruit and veggies are hung from a tree branch. Giraffes use their agile tongues to reach into the ball and nab what they want. When the ball swings, the task gets even tougher!

The smarter an animal is, the more challenge it needs. Super-smarties like parrots and chimps might be given their food in locked boxes. They have to go through a series of unfamiliar steps—like turning keys or sliding levers—in the right order to free the treat. Puzzles like these make feeding time more fun than, well, a barrel of monkeys!

DIGGER'S DELIGHT

YOU WILL NEED
- 1 ripe banana, smushed
- 1 cup (250 mL) cooked oatmeal, cooled
- ⅓ cup (85 mL) peanut butter
- 1 tbsp. (15 mL) honey
- ⅓ cup (85 mL) Hawaiian Punch or other fruit-flavored drink
- log with deep hole in it, or a hollow piece of bamboo

1. Mix first four ingredients together.
2. Add Hawaiian Punch one spoonful at a time until mixture is the consistency of paste.
3. Spoon the mixture into the log or bamboo. Allow it to harden. Chimps will enjoy trying to dig out the tasty treat using their fingers or sticks all day long!

Meet a Zoo Nutritionist

Who: Andrea Fidgett, Nutritionist

Where: Chester Zoo, Upton-by-Chester, England

Favorite part of the job: I never stop learning about species new to me—their ecology, their habits, and how they settle into the zoo.

Most challenging part of the job: When an individual animal is not eating, and you've tried everything you would normally try, and they can't tell you what's wrong. It becomes a real team effort, involving the nutritionist, keepers, and even vets to help the animal get its appetite back.

Andrea's typical lunch: Homemade salads in summer; hearty warming soups in winter.

POLLY WANNA PUZZLE?
Are you as smart as a parrot? Figure out the steps required to move the "treat" through the locked-box maze so it can pop out the door. Answer is on page 32.

Picky, Pickier, Pickiest!

Pandas only eat bamboo. Koalas stick to leaves from the eucalyptus tree. How do zoos cater to these choosiest of chewers? At the Lone Pine Koala Sanctuary in Australia, two leaf cutters on staff collect 1,100 lb. (500 kg) of eucalyptus branches from their plantations every day. The branches are brought back to the zoo in supersized wheeled bins.

On site, the leafy branches are put into pots filled with water to keep them fresh and juicy. The keepers then attach the pots to the animals' perching poles. That way, koalas can munch all day long without coming down. Talk about "potluck"!

EAT. NAP. REPEAT.

Every koala has its favorite varieties of eucalyptus. A koala might prefer one species, while snubbing another. Keepers need to remember which critter prefers which kind of eucalyptus. And even the fussiest of fussbudgets likes a change of pace. Every now and then, koalas may go wild and nibble on a tea leaf!

Eucalyptus leaves don't provide a lot of energy. That's why koalas sleep 18 to 20 hours a day. They also don't store body fat. That roly-poly paunch? It's really a colossal digestive system!

FEEDING A SICK KOALA

According to koala keeper Karen Nilsson from the Lone Pine Koala Sanctuary, sick koalas are a *lot* of work! Just like people, they become even fussier eaters when they are ill. Keepers have to collect the tastiest leaves they can find and offer them by hand, one at a time. Extremely sick koalas might get a specially prepared treat, like delicious eucalyptus Presto Pesto Sauce, to help speed them back to health.

PRESTO PESTO SAUCE— KOALA STYLE

Serve koalas this easy-to-eat treat when they're under the weather. No pillow-plumping required.

YOU WILL NEED

1 cup (250 mL)
eucalyptus leaves

¼ cup (62.5 mL)
soy-based
infant formula

1. Chop eucalyptus leaves in a blender until very fine.

2. Add formula to the chopped leaves until the mixture is the consistency of cake batter.

3. Hand-feed to sick koalas from a large syringe.

MAKE IT FRESH . . . AND FRENCH

Koalas aren't nature's only picky eaters. In the wild, a giant panda's diet is about 99% bamboo. But bamboo doesn't grow in Austria, and that's a problem for panda keepers at Vienna's Schönbrunn Zoo. The solution? Every other week, 4 tons (4,000 kg) of bamboo is driven to the zoo all the way from the South of France.

Seafood Special

At the Birch Aquarium in La Jolla, California, the marine menu changes with the tides. The aquarium's seafood arrives frozen and is stored in a giant walk-in freezer. Each night, staff members transfer about 25 lb. (11 kg) of it to the fish food refrigerator to thaw. The next morning, they simply chop the food with a knife. Then the prepped food goes into plastic containers and is taken to the tanks.

The fish might be broadcast-fed, which means food is strewn randomly through the water. Some, though, are target-fed, which means they eat from specific feeding poles. This lets the keepers track the health of each animal more carefully. Sick fish may even be target-fed with tongs to make sure that their medicine isn't eaten by another animal.

ALL-YOU-CAN-EAT ALGAE BUFFET

Plant eaters like parrot fish get "algae logs" to gnaw on. These are made up of different types of powdered algae (underwater plants) mixed with vitamins and water. Fish will swarm an algae log like people crowd around a buffet table! Algae also grow naturally throughout the tanks, providing good grazing for fish that prefer to dine solo.

KELP TANK GOULASH

This toothsome treat is delivered daily to fish housed in the Birch Aquarium's two-storey, 70,000 gal. (265 L) kelp tank, which recreates an underwater seaweed forest.

YOU WILL NEED

handful of large krill
handful of chopped clams
10 coarsely chopped squid
15 coarsely chopped smelt
4 coarsely chopped mackerel, heads and intestines removed

1. Mix all ingredients in a bucket.
2. Sprinkle "goulash" throughout the kelp tank to feed the leopard sharks, Garibaldi fish, eels, barracudas, giant sea bass, and more.

Save Our Seas–Please!

One of the most important jobs at the Birch Aquarium is conservation. The aquarium helps care for sea animals that are in danger. It also teaches visitors about the ocean and its ecosystems. The more we know about the ocean, the more likely we are to keep it healthy!

One key way people can help the ocean is to avoid eating endangered seafood species. But how do you know if the fish in your fish-wich is a safe choice? The Monterey Bay Aquarium has prepared a guide to help you figure it out. It divides seafood into three categories. "Best choices" include seafood that is caught, farmed, or managed in ways that are not harmful to the overall health of the species or to the environment. "Good alternatives" are *usually* caught or farmed in acceptable ways. The "Avoid" category includes seafood that is endangered, farmed, or caught in ways that harm the environment.

Here's how to check the status of your fish-wich:

- **Download** a guide to your area or an app at the Monterey Bay Aquarium's website: www.seafoodwatch.org.

- **Check** a specific type of seafood individually at the Monterey Bay Aquarium website: www.seafoodwatch.org.

- **Ask** the person serving the fish what it is. Remember, it's always wise to know what you are eating and where it came from!

Big Eaters

Extra-large animals can go through tons of food—literally. African elephants can eat 660 lb. (300 kg) in a single day. Most of that food comes in the form of hay. But keepers may also feed elephants up to 15 lb. (7 kg) of fruit and vegetables a day. Melons, pineapples, pears, celery, parsley, lettuce, cabbage, kale, tomatoes, potatoes, onions, beets, sugar cane, apples, sweet potatoes, and bananas all figure on the menu.

Large herbivores also eat "browse"—whole shrubs or trees, complete with leaves, bark, seeds, and stems. Tearing up and chewing the tough fibers is good for their teeth and digestion. It's also lots of fun! At Tennessee's Nashville Zoo, favorite forms of browse include hackberry, sweetgum, and maple trees, as well as bamboo.

Big appetites like these mean big expenses for zoos. At the Elephant Sanctuary in Tennessee, for example, the grocery bill adds up to almost $1,000 per month, per elephant!

KEEPING FIT, ELEPHANT-STYLE

In zoos, big eaters might not get as much exercise as they would in the wild. Like people, zoo animals can pack on the pounds if they overeat or don't get enough exercise. That's not good for their health.

At the Fresno Chaffee Zoo in California, an elephant named Shaunzi weighed in at a whopping 10,245 lb. (4,650 kg). That's too much, even for an elephant. So zookeepers limited the foods Shaunzi ate and switched her from high-calorie fruit like apples to lower-calorie foods like carrots. They also added more exercise to her day. Keepers buried treats so she'd have to dig them out with her tusks—much like elephants do in the wild. After all these efforts, Shaunzi lost about 1,110 lb. (500 kg)!

Did You Know?

When you eat as much as an elephant, you wind up pooping a lot, too. Shaunzi produces over 100 lb. (45 kg) of poo a day! Her zoo came up with a novel way to get rid of it—they sell it! Zoo Poo is sold by the quart (liter) as compost to local gardeners. Elephant poo has also been used to make 100% organic paper!

ELEPHANT-SLIMMING FRUIT FANDANGO

Elephants burn a lot of calories to get this snack out of its "wrapper."

YOU WILL NEED

6 apples

6 oranges

6 bananas

6 carrots

2 pieces sugar cane

1 metal barrel with holes poked in its sides

1. Quarter the apples and oranges. Halve the bananas and carrots.

2. Place fruit, carrot, and sugar cane pieces into barrel.

3. Serve barrel to elephant as an intriguing treat. Is it a musical instrument? (Bang, BANG!) Or perhaps it's a rattle? Inquisitive elephants stay amused for hours!

Treat Days!

It's May 24, and that means it's party time for Anastasia and Katya, two rare Siberian tigers at the Seneca Park Zoo in Rochester, New York. To celebrate, zookeepers put up decorations and sing "Happy Birthday." And of course, there are delicious treats for all the animals—and their human guests, too!

Animals don't celebrate birthdays in the wild, but hosting a celebration with special events and foods adds excitement to what can be a routine life for zoo animals. Celebrations also bring visitors to zoos—and attention to the issues that zoos want to highlight, like conservation. Of course, celebrating a birthday is an extra-big deal if, like Anastasia and Katya, the guest of honor belongs to an endangered species.

TIGER'S BIRTHDAY CUPCAKE

Tigers will roar for more!

YOU WILL NEED

8½ cups (2 L) animal blood (cow, sheep, pig, or goat)

round plastic container

1 piece horse tail or oxtail, bone in

1 large bunch catnip

1. Pour the blood into the round plastic container. Freeze until partially set.

2. Stick the tail piece into the partially set blood so it stands upright. The knobby end should look like a cherry on the top of a cupcake.

3. Spread the catnip around the cupcake like icing and push down into the blood. Return to freezer until fully frozen.

4. Remove the frozen cake from the container and serve to the birthday tiger with a rousing chorus of "Happy Birthday."

A YEAR-LONG PARTY!

Birthdays aren't the only special occasions celebrated at zoos. Lucky animals celebrate special occasions all year round.

- At Hawaii's Honolulu Zoo, the Easter Bunny delivers treat-filled baskets to the animals. Gibbons also go on Easter egg hunts. They gobble the eggs whole—shells and all.

- Diwali, the Hindu festival of lights, is prime party time for animals at the Lucknow Zoo in India. Elephants, rhinos, and hippos light up when they receive a festive treat of bananas and jaggery (a coarse brown sugar). Bears celebrate with honeyed kheer, a kind of rice pudding.

- The Chinese Mid-Autumn Festival is an especially happy time for pandas in China's zoos. They receive gifts of traditional moon cakes—made extra-large and with non-traditional stuffings of favorite panda foods, like bamboo leaves.

- At the Lowry Park Zoo in Tampa, Florida, primates celebrate Halloween by participating in a pumpkin toss! All the animals get to eat the jack-o'-lantern as their prize.

- At Christmastime at the Atlanta Zoo in Georgia, the gift for large herbivores is the Christmas tree itself. It makes for tasty browse!

For the Birds

Birds come in all shapes and sizes. They eat a wide variety of foods, too. That presents a special set of challenges to zookeepers. At the National Aviary in Washington, DC, birds are fed at different heights of the enclosure. Some find their meals up high in the tree canopy, while others must root them out in the shrubs below.

Keepers also separate different kinds of foods, like meat, fish, and fruit, so birds with different diets don't dine together. This, plus positive reinforcement training (teaching the birds how to behave, and giving them rewards when they do), keeps conflicts out of the cage.

Did You Know?

Birds don't have teeth. So how do they "chew" their food? They have a very muscular stomach called a gizzard. The gizzard squeezes and mashes the food inside it. To help the gizzard do its work, birds occasionally eat pebbles or bits of sand. The rocks and grit stay in the gizzard and chop food up just like your teeth do.

APPLE SURPRISE!

For white-headed buffalo weaver birds and green woodhoopoes.

YOU WILL NEED

an apple   20 mealworms

1. Slice off the top quarter of the apple and core the rest.

2. Cut four pencil-sized holes in the sides of the apple.

3. Fill cored apple with 20 mealworms. Replace top.

4. Secure food treat in a tree for feeding.

HOW TO EAT LIKE A BIRD

Pelicans at Arizona's Phoenix Zoo prefer fish. When a special bell is rung, the birds start to gather, squawking and jostling for best position. Then keepers toss small fish like herring or smelt for the birds to catch midair.

Lorikeets at the Lone Pine Koala Sanctuary in Australia get a mix of nectar, oats and other cereals, and vitamins. They lap the mixture from feeding bowls with their brush-tipped tongues.

Ostriches, the largest birds on earth, are omnivores. At the San Diego Zoo in California, they eat vitamin-enriched bird pellets, browse, and tasty veggies like carrots and broccoli.

Hornbills prefer colorful fruit salads of chopped apples, pears, papayas, grapes, and blueberries, with a crunchy garnish: a light sprinkling of mealworms and locusts.

Problems in Captivity

While zookeepers do their best to feed and care for their charges, they can't fully recreate natural conditions. Kept in enclosures, foragers can't travel to find foods that ripen at different seasons. Carnivores can't hunt a range of prey like they do on the plains or in a rain forest. As a result, even the best zoo diets can be more limited than an animal's wild diet.

In some cases, zookeepers don't fully know what their charges eat in the wild. Some, like the clouded leopard, are secretive and not easy to observe in their natural habitat. Keepers can only make a best guess at what to serve these mysterious creatures. In other cases, zookeepers know exactly what foods an animal prefers, but they can't get it. For example, they might not be able to serve fresh browse to large herbivores in the winter.

Zookeepers work hard to figure out how to keep their animals healthy despite these challenges because—for some animals—a zoo diet is better than no diet at all. Many species in the wild are threatened by habitat loss or poaching (illegal hunting). For them, zoos provide a safe place to live and reproduce, representing hope for survival.

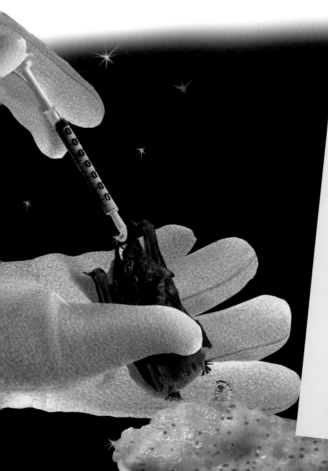

MIDNIGHT MEALWORM MUSH

At Bat World, a sanctuary in Texas for orphaned or injured bats, feeding time presents a different kind of challenge. In the wild, nocturnal insect-eating bats nab dinner on the fly, but they can't catch flying bugs in an enclosure. So at Bat World, keepers carefully feed mealworms to each animal by hand.

YOU WILL NEED

1 cup (500 mL) mealworms   vitamins

1. Blend mealworms and vitamins into a soft mush.
2. Place mixture in a small syringe.
3. Warm syringe in hot but not scalding water.
4. Hold bat securely. Give it a tiny drop of food every seven seconds, or when the bat indicates it's ready by chewing on the tip of the syringe.

HOME IS WHERE THE HEART IS

Zoos can't always provide a good long-term home. Some animals, like great white sharks, cannot be kept in captivity. Scientists believe the sharks need to swim over huge ranges to capture enough food. The animals also become aggressive when kept in tanks for even short periods of time.

Elephants can also be difficult to care for. These social animals need the company of many other elephants. Yet most zoos can't afford to keep more than a few elephants at a time. The animals also suffer from a lack of space. And in cold climates,

winter weather limits their outdoor time. Even with excellent care, elephants tend to live shorter lives in captivity than they do in the wild.

For these reasons, three elephants from the Toronto Zoo–Iringa, Toka, and Thika–were relocated to PAWS ARK 2000 Sanctuary in San Andreas, California, in 2013. The sanctuary is more like their native habitat in Africa. The eldest, Iringa, died in 2015. Toka and Thika seem happy in their new home.

Be a Bestie to the Beasties!

Feeding animals healthy zoo food is only one part of a zookeeper's job. There are many different ways to take care of animals—both inside and outside the zoo! Get started now with these animal-friendly tips:

- **Find out more:** Read books and magazines and watch television shows and documentaries that focus on animals and animal conservation.

- **Adopt an animal:** Organizations like the World Wildlife Fund offer programs where your donation can help support a wild or zoo animal, and help fund future conservation.

- **Volunteer:** Join a local cleanup effort that helps restore wild spaces like rivers or parks. For example, every year, residents of Toronto, Ontario, get together to cleanup the Don, the river that runs through the city. Similar efforts take place in New York, London, and other cities around the world.

- **Get outside:** The easiest way to learn about animals and the natural world is by spending time at a local park or in your own backyard. If you can, get wilder by hiking or camping in a national park or animal preserve.

- **Create safe local habitats:** Help the wild animals that live right in your neighborhood by building birdfeeders full of healthy seeds or planting butterfly gardens full of native plants.

- **Spread the word:** Tell everyone you know about the need for animal conservation, and encourage them to join the effort to keep animals safe.

- **Take care of the planet:** Reduce the amount of stuff you consume, reuse whatever you can, and recycle as much as possible. Remember, human beings are also animals. So taking care of the planet takes care of us, too.

Did You Know?

Our species, *Homo sapiens*, is found on a branch of the animal family tree called primates. Our closest relatives are the great apes, and include chimpanzees and bonobos. We are also related to gorillas, orangutans, gibbons, and even lemurs!

Glossary

Browse: whole shrubs or trees—complete with leaves, bark, and seeds—fed to large herbivores

Calorie: a unit of measure of heat energy; commonly used to describe the amount of energy stored in foods

Conservation: the act of preserving, protecting, and/or restoring the natural environment, including ecosystems, vegetation, and wildlife

Diet: the foods that a person or animal normally eats; also a specialized, restricted food plan for achieving a goal, like weight loss

Endangered: at serious risk of extinction; vulnerable

Extinct: having no more living members; no longer in existence

Forager: one who searches for plant-based foods to eat

Larva: the young, often worm-like stage of certain types of animals that hatch from eggs, like insects and crustaceans

Nocturnal: active at night

Nutrient: the parts of food (such as protein, fats, and sugars) that provide the essential materials for living things to survive and grow

Nutritionist: an expert on how food and nutrition can affect health

Predator: an animal that survives by killing and eating other animals

Prey: an animal that is hunted and killed by other animals to provide a source of food

Sanctuary: a place that offers safety

Answers to puzzles

PAGES 4–5

Panda–Bamboo   Anteater–Ants   Sloth–Salad   Otter–Crab   Chimp–Termites in a Mound   Owl–Mouse

PAGE 17

Remove the pink key (1). Then unscrew the red-tipped screw (2) and pull out the green cylinder (3). Twist the red button (4) so that the slot runs vertically, matching the thin metal rod. Remove the red button (5), slide the deadbolt to the right (6), and eat the cracker!

Index